TRISTIA

Осип Эмильевич Мандельштам в 1914 году
(С редкой фотографии поэта)

OSIP
MANDELSTAM

TRISTIA

TRANSLATED BY
BRUCE McCLELLAND

STATION
HILL
1987

Published by Station Hill Press, Inc., Barrytown, NY 12507 with grateful acknowledgment to the National Endowment for the Arts, a federal agency in Washington, DC, and the New York State Council on the Arts, for partial financial support of this project.

Distributed by The Talman Co., 150 Fifth Avenue, New York, NY 10011.

Produced by the Institute for Publishing Arts, Barrytown, NY 12507, a not-for-profit, tax-exempt organization.

Earlier versions of most of these poems appeared in the anthology *The Silver Age of Russian Culture*, published by Ardis Press (Ann Arbor: 1971), printed here by permission. In addition, a brief selection of poems was printed in *The Bard Review*, Benjamin LaFarge, editor.

The Russian text photographically reproduces the original Petrograd edition of 1922 (republished in facsimile by Ardis Press, Ann Arbor: 1972). The central rectangle on the present cover reproduces the original cover art of M. V. Dobuzhinsky (1875-1957). The original colophon translates as: "Cover and [printer's] mark by M. V. Dobuzhinsky. Typography by Zinaburg & Co. in Berlin in 1922 for the Publisher 'Petropolis.' "

The translator wishes to thank all those who in any way assisted in bringing these poems into English, especially Michael Minihan, who first pointed out the work of Mandelstam; Justus Rosenberg, who assisted with the Russian; and Deborah Breeding and Robert Kelly, who were honest and patient from the very beginning.

Designed by Susan Quasha.

Library of Congress Cataloging in Publication Data

Mandel'shtam, Osip, 1891-1938.
    Tristia.

    Translated from the Russian.
    "Reprinted with permission of Ardis Publishers from The Silver Age of Russian Culture (Ann Arbor, 1971) which published an earlier version of the present translation of Bruce McClelland"—T.p. verso.
    1. Mandel'shtam, Osip, 1891-1938—Translations, English. I. McClelland, Bruce. II. Title.
PG3476.M355A246 1987   891.71'3   886-32305
ISBN 0-88268-041-2

Manufactured in the United States of America.

2-29-88 — MW-51490

For Michael Minihan and Justus Rosenberg, after all.

TABLE OF CONTENTS (RUSSIAN)

TABLE OF CONTENTS (ENGLISH)

PREFACE

Osip Emilievich Mandelstam was born near the beginning of the new age in Russia, an era whose most momentous achievement was the Great October Revolution of 1917. In 1891, the assassination of Alexander II was ten years past, and as the century's end drew nearer, there arose the expectation of some enormous change, one which would at last rectify the social and political injustices of Russia's long dynasties of tsars.

This dawn of anticipation was marked in poetry by a foreboding sense of the coming upheaval as something of a mystical event. Ambivalence concerning the effects of such a wrenching change appears in the art of the day, where the beginnings of socialist realism struggle against the otherworldliness of the Russian Symbolist poets and philosophers Blok, Bely, Merezhkovsky, Soloviev.

The Symbolists in particular were initially optimistic, even amid their great uncertainty about the fate of valued cultural structures. A sort of ill-defined gnosticism, or at least a Russified theosophy, in which the embodiment of the positive force behind the forthcoming transformation is the figure of the divine and eternally feminine Sophia, became the aesthetic base for a poetry filled with allusiveness and marked by a reliance upon a limited stock of "symbols."

These symbols were to be understood not so much as metaphoric substitutes as actual *correspondences*. By understanding the relationships and forces between the symbols within the poetry, the reader gets an intimation of the relationships that obtain at higher levels of experience.

While such a sensibility is a perfect consequence of both the political and spiritual conditions of late Nineteenth Century Russia—and it should be understood that some facets of this attitude were very nearly apocalyptic in tone—by the time Mandelstam was old enough to be aware of the poetics of the immediately preceding generation, the Symbolists' insistence upon the import of their correspondences had grown tiresome. Even Blok's well-known vision of the heavenly 'Unknown Lady' (*Neznakomka*), originally pure and luminous, eventually becomes sullied to such an extent that She takes on the aspect of a prostitute.

Regardless of the distortions within Blok's private life that led to that degraded projection (and it may be that the archetype entails its shadow), the deterioration of the Image, the inability to maintain it against compromise, becomes symptomatic of the whole state of Symbolism by the beginning of this century's second decade. The collapse of the system, due as much as anything to a growing rigidity of its language and a too heavy reliance upon technique, was signaled by a preponderance of an all-too-familiar set of images and concerns. Even the earlier prosodic experiments of Bely, in which the sounds of the words clanging together were to be appreciated for their approximation to music (deemed the highest spiritual art), gave way to a hunger for a poetry that could deal more effectively with the realities of Russian culture at the beginning of the new century.

Mandelstam, then, came into his poetic maturity at just that point when the archetypal images of the Symbolists needed to be re-visioned. The Symbolists themselves were aware of it. An editorial in the final number of the Symbolist journal Vesy (Scales) in 1909 stated,

> We do not wish to say by this that the Symbolist movement has died, that Symbolism has ceased to play the role of the watch-word of our age.... But tomorrow the same word will become another watch-word, will burn with a different flame, and it already burns in a different way above us.

Ordinarily, the self-consciousness of literary movements— definite *Isms* in this case—does not extend to such clear recognition of their own demise. But it was a *time* of Isms, and apparently the passing away of one called for the immediate emergence of another.

The major, although not the only, replacement for Russian Symbolism, the new "watch-word," was Acmeism, a name which eventually came to be associated with Osip Mandelstam more than with its founder, the poet Nikolai Gumilev.

Gumilev, the husband of another significant Acmeist poet, Anna Akhmatova, was the original, if not the most profound, theoretician of Acmeism. A scant three years following the official extinction of the Symbolists in Vesy, Gumilev proposed both the name and the central theme of this new movement:

> To replace Symbolism there is a new movement, which, whatever it is called—Acmeism (from the word ἀκμή—the highest degree of something, the flower, the time of flowering), or Adamism (a manfully firm, clear view of life),—demands, in any case, greater balance of powers and a more exact knowledge of the relationships between subject and object than there was in Symbolism.... The first thing that Acmeism can answer is to point out that the unknowable, by the very meaning of the word cannot be known. The second, that all endeavors in that direction are unchaste. The whole beauty,

the whole sacred meaning of the stars lies in the fact that they are infinitely far from earth.

It was to this kind of poetics that Mandelstam was drawn in his mid-twenties. Gumilev and the other Acmeists, having identified the cornerstones of the new school as Shakespeare, Rabelais, Villon, and Théophile Gautier, had constructed a stance relative to the strong but waning influence of the earlier movement which suited Mandelstam's temperament and credentials. The essence of this stance is aptly described by Clarence Brown:

> Equipped with his knowledge of human psychology and physiology, the Acmeist was to 'adjust'—not in gloomy resignation, but joyfully—to reality, and in the strictness of self-imposed forms write balanced, clear poems about it all. [*Mandelstam*, p. 141]

Obviously, if Mandelstam had himself not been capable of raising this platform to a new level, it would be difficult to make the claim that I am about to make, namely that the poems of *Tristia* comprise the acme of Acmeism, which in turn became a literary philosophy whose concerns resonate with many issues in contemporary poetic discourse.† For while Mandelstam lived comfortably with "the strictness of self-imposed forms," at the same time he certainly did not simply "adjust" to reality. Rather, he invested poetry itself with such a high degree of substantiality that for him (and for us) it was capable of *penetrating* reality—breaking the glass of illusion in a way that all the theosophical incantations of the Symbolists never could.

---

† Although this is not the place to examine the relationship between Mandelstam's elaborate poetics and the development of Western poetic traditions, it is useful to note once again (Clarence Brown mentions it in his critical biography, *Mandelstam*) the similarity between certain tenets of Acmeism and Imagism. Consider Ezra Pound's own view of Symbolism:

> Imagisme is not Symbolism. The Symbolists dealt in "association," that is, in a sort of allusion, almost of allegory. They degraded the symbol to the status of a word. They made it a form of metonomy...the symbolists' *symbols* have a fixed value, like the numbers in arithmetic, like 1, 2, and 7. The imagiste's images have a variable significance, like the signs *a*, *b*, and *x* in algebra.
>
> Moreover, one does not want to be called a symbolist, because symbolism has usually been associated with mushy technique. [*Gaudier Brzeska*, p. 97]

The title of Mandelstam's first book *Kamen'* (Stone) (1913) suggests the solidity of the Mandelstamian poem. But in that first book, the stone's quality of heaviness—the heart—is more visible than its quality of stability, that which makes it useful as a material for building. It is as if Mandelstam has identified, by the time of his first book, the objective reality that true poetry can have, but has not yet learned of its transformative power. For it is of stone that the Gothic cathedral—an ever-present image in Mandelstam's later critical writings—is built; an organic "physiology," constructed from a common participation in the "fight against emptiness." "The fine arrow of the Gothic belltower," he maintains in his manifesto "The Morning of Acmeism," "is angry, for the whole idea of it is to stab the sky, to reproach it for being empty."

If the poems of the present collection transcend those of his earlier book, it is because the stones—the words—have been so assembled that we are able to perceive the divine physiognomy within the architected space:

> And in the stone arches of the Assumption
> I see high, arched brows.

> From the ramparts, fortified with archangels,
> I surveyed the city from a marvelous height.

The pinnacle constructed by this labor is, of course, *acme*. *Acme*, for Mandelstam, must have meant a position, an actual perceptive situation, from which one can see directly into the real. From this vantage, Mandelstam is able to observe (and thereby report upon) the *city*—grand plan of the *meso*cosm—in a fashion that the Symbolists, their attentions fastened upon the macrocosm, could not.

It is hard to talk about Mandelstam without resorting to some kind of spatial, usually architectural, metaphor—not just because of the clarity of Mandelstam's own elaboration of such metaphors, but also because of his enormous awareness. The city—Petersburg, for Mandelstam—exists in time, a net of nodes which connect all history to all geography at any event. He "surveys the city from a marvelous height."

It is this perspective, obtained through Mandelstam's patient and careful use of language, that enables him to retain his artistic integrity in the face of the very historical forces that were to conspire against him. Mandelstam's unshakeable faith in his art, based primarily upon the vision obtained from it, prevented him from sacrificing the Word rather than his life.

Tristia—'sad things,' 'sorrows'—is the condition of these poems not because of some personal ego loss. Rather, the title of this collection is apt because the *acme* as the high point is a place of isolation—not desolation. The sadness of Mandelstam—a Jew fascinated his entire life with the Christian myth and its cultural effects—in the years of war and chaos is the sadness of Christ surveying from the cross the mass of spectators who were unaware of their own involvement in history. It is the sadness of the alienated true poet, the one who has mastered language and its powers only to discover that his voice has not been heard above the rush of history's wave.

It was a sad time. These are not 'sad' poems, as a whole, or if so, not nearly so sad as those in *Stone*, which falls prey too often to that "emptiness" that Mandelstam's version of Acmeism intended to fight. But collectively, they convey the pain of an isolation caused by the maintenance of absolute integrity, which in his case led to his involuntary exile and destruction.

The beautiful and oft-cited title poem provides better than any critical statement the key to the problem of acmeism, the problem of Mandelstam:

> Who knows, at the mention of 'farewell,'
> What separation awaits us,
> What the cockscrow augurs
> When flames glow on the acropolis,
> And in the dawn of some new life
> While an ox chews lazily in his shed,
> Why the cock, herald of new life,
> Beats his wings on the town's walls?

TRISTIA

— Какъ этихъ покрывалъ и этого убора
Мнѣ пышность тяжела средь моего позора!

    — Будетъ въ каменной Трезенѣ
    Знаменитая бѣда,
    Царской лѣстницы ступени
    Покраснѣютъ отъ стыда,
    . . . .
    . . . .
    И для матери влюбленной
    Солнце черное взойдетъ.

— О, если бъ ненависть въ груди моей кипѣла —
Но, видите, само признанье съ устъ слетѣло.

    — Чернымъ пламенемъ Федра горитъ
    Среди бѣлаго дня.
    Погребальный факелъ горитъ
    Среди бѣлаго дня.
    Бойся матери, ты, Ипполитъ:
    Федра — ночь — тебя сторожитъ
    Среди бѣлаго дня.

— Любовью черною я солнце запятнала,
Смерть охладитъ мой пылъ изъ чистаго фіала...

    — Мы боимся, мы не смѣемъ
    Горю царскому помочь.
    Уязвленная Тезеемъ
    На него напала ночь.
    Мы же, пѣснью похоронной
    Провожая мертвыхъ въ домъ,
    Страсти дикой и безсонной
    Солнце черное уймемъ.

    1916

—No matter how I concealed them, even the
splendor of this attire is burdensome amidst my shame.—

    —There will be a famous calamity in stony Troezen,
    the royal staircase will grow red with disgrace

   .   .   .   .

   .   .   .   .

    and for the mother in love,
    the black sun will rise.

—O, if hate would boil in my breast—
but see, the confession itself
has fallen from my lips.

    —Phedre burns in black flames
        in broad white daylight.
    The funeral torch fumes
        in broad white daylight.
    Dread your mother, Hippolytus:
    Phedre—night—lies in wait for you
        in broad white day. [1]

—I have stained the sun with blackened love...
Death from a phial will cool my ardor—

.   .   .   .

    —We are afraid, we do not dare
    to help in the king's time of need.
    Wounded by Theseus, night
    fell upon him. But we,
    who with funeral songs bring home the dead
    will possess the black sun
    in wild and sleepless passion.

ЗВѢРИНЕЦЪ.

1

Отверженное слово „миръ"
Въ началѣ оскорбленной эры;
Свѣтильникъ въ глубинѣ пещеры
И воздухъ горныхъ странъ — эфиръ;
Эфиръ, которымъ не сумѣли,
Не захотѣли мы дышать.
Козлинымъ голосомъ, опять,
Поютъ косматыя свирѣли.

2

Пока ягнята и волы
На тучныхъ пастбищахъ водились
И дружелюбные садились
На плечи сонныхъ скалъ орлы, —
Германецъ выкормилъ орла,
И левъ британцу покорился,
И галльскій гребень появился
Изъ пѣтушинаго хохла.

3

А нынѣ завладѣлъ дикарь
Священной палицей Геракла,
И черная земля изсякла,
Неблагодарная, какъ встарь.
Я палочку возьму сухую,
Огонь добуду изъ нея.
Пускай уходитъ въ ночь глухую
Мной всполошенное звѣрье.

4

Пѣтухъ, и левъ, и темно-бурый
Орелъ, и ласковый медвѣдь —
Мы для войны построимъ клѣть,
Звѣриныя пригрѣемъ шкуры.
А я пою вино временъ,
Источникъ рѣчи италійской,
И, въ колыбели праарійской,
Славянскій и германскій ленъ.

THE MENAGERIE

1

The rejected word "peace"
At the beginning of an outraged era;
A church lamp in a catacomb
And the air of celestial regions
An ether we did not want,
Or know how, to breathe.
Again, with a goat-voice,
The shaggy reed-pipes sing.

2

While sheep and oxen grazed
On fertile pastures,
And friendly eagles perched
On the shoulders of sleepy crags,—
A German raised an eagle,
A lion submitted to a Briton,
And a Gallic comb appeared
From a rooster's crest.

3

But now the savage has captured
The sacred mace of Heracles,
The black earth has dried up,
Ungrateful, as before.
I will take away the withered staff
And draw the fire from it;
Let the frightened beast go away
With me into the deaf night.

4

The cock, the lion, the dark brown
Eagle, the affectionate bear—
We shall build a chamber for war,
And warm the wild beasts' hides.
But I sing the wine of the times—
The source of Italic speech—
And in a Great-Aryan cradle,
Slavonic and Germanic flax!

5

Италія, тебѣ не лѣнь
Тревожить Рима колесницы,
Съ кудахтаньемъ домашней птицы
Перелетѣвъ черезъ плетень?
И ты, сосѣдка, не взыщи:
Орелъ топорщится и злится.
Что, если для твоей пращи
Тяжелый камень не годится?

6

Въ звѣринцѣ заперевъ звѣрей,
Мы успокоимся надолго,
И станетъ полноводнѣй Волга,
И рейнская струя свѣтлѣй.
И умудренный человѣкъ
Почтитъ невольно чужестранца,
Какъ полубога, буйствомъ танца,
На берегахъ великихъ рѣкъ!

1916

5

Italy, is it not indolence for you
To disturb the chariots of Rome,
With the clucking of a domestic bird
Flying across your fence?
And you, neighbor, don't be hard on them;
The eagle spreads its wings in anger.
What if for your sling
A heavy stone is of no use?

6

While the beasts are in the menagerie,
We are content a while,
The Volga stays at high tide,
The Rhine's current grows brighter—
The wise man will unwillingly honor
A foreigner as a demi-god
With the exuberance of a dance
On the shores of great rivers.

Въ разноголосицѣ дѣвическаго хора
Всѣ церкви нѣжныя поютъ на голосъ свой,
И въ дугахъ каменныхъ Успенскаго собора
Мнѣ брови чудятся, высокія, дугой.

И съ укрѣпленнаго архангелами вала
Я городъ озиралъ на чудной высотѣ.
Въ стѣнахъ Акрополя печаль меня снѣдала,
По русскомъ имени и русской красотѣ.

Не диво ль дивное, что вертоградъ намъ снится,
Гдѣ рѣютъ голуби въ горячей синевѣ,
Что православные крюки поетъ черница:
Успенье нѣжное — Флоренція въ Москвѣ.

И пятиглавые московскіе соборы
Съ ихъ итальянскою и русскою душой
Напоминаютъ мнѣ — явленіе Авроры,
Но съ русскимъ именемъ и въ шубкѣ мѣховой.

1916

Every church sings its own soft part
In the polyphony of a girl's choir,
And in the stone arches of the Assumption
I see high, arched brows.

From the ramparts, fortified with archangels,
I surveyed the city from a marvelous height.
Within the walls of this acropolis, I was consumed
With sorrow for the Russian name, for Russian beauty.

Isn't it strangely wonderful, we dream
Of an orchard, soaring pigeons in the hot blue sky,
A nun is singing the litany:
Tender Assumption: Florence in Moscow.

The five-domed cathedrals of Moscow,
With their Italian and Russian souls
Remind me of Aurora, but with a
Russian name, and in a fur coat.

На розвальняхъ, уложенныхъ соломой,
Едва прикрытые рогожей роковой,
Отъ Воробьевыхъ горъ до церковки знакомой
Мы ѣхали огромною Москвой.

А въ Угличѣ играютъ дѣти въ бабки,
И пахнетъ хлѣбъ, оставленный въ печи.
По улицамъ меня везутъ безъ шапки,
И теплятся въ часовнѣ три свѣчи.

Не три свѣчи горѣли, а три встрѣчи,
Одну изъ нихъ самъ Богъ благословилъ,
Четвертой не бывать, — а Римъ далече,
И никогда онъ Рима не любилъ.
Ныряли сани въ черные ухабы,
И возвращался съ гульбища народъ.
Худые мужики и злыя бабы
Лущили сѣмя у воротъ.

Сырая даль отъ птичьихъ стай чернѣла,
И связанныя руки затекли.
Царевича везутъ—нѣмѣетъ страшно тѣло,
И рыжую солому подожгли.

1916

On a sleigh, padded with straw,
Barely covered by the fated mat,
From the Vorobevy hills to the familiar chapel
We rode towards enormous Muscovy.

But in Uglich, [2] the children play knucklebones,
And it smells of bread still in the oven.
They carry me along the street without my hat;
In the oratory three candles burn. [3]

Not three candles glowing—three meetings. [4]
One consecrated by God Himself.
A fourth would never be, but Rome is far—
And He was never fond of Rome.

The sled dashed through black ruts,
People jumped back from the street.
Wretched peasants with their angry wives
Were bowled over at the gates.

The damp distance blackened with flocks of birds,
The bound hands [5] swelled. They carry the Tsarevich,
His body grows terribly numb,
They set fire to the reddened straw.

СОЛОМИНКА.

I

Когда, соломинка, ты спишь въ огромной спальнѣ
И ждешь, безсонная, чтобъ, важенъ и высокъ,
Спокойной тяжестью — что можетъ быть печальнѣй —
На вѣки чуткія спустился потолокъ,

Соломка звонкая, соломинка сухая,
Всю смерть ты выпила и сдѣлалась нѣжнѣй,
Сломалась милая соломка неживая,
Не Саломея, нѣтъ, соломинка скорѣй.

Въ часы безсонницы предметы тяжелѣе,
Какъ будто меньше ихъ — такая тишина —
Мерцаютъ въ зеркалѣ подушки, чуть бѣлѣя,
И въ кругломъ омутѣ кровать отражена.

Нѣтъ, не соломинка въ торжественномъ атласѣ,
Въ огромной комнатѣ надъ черною Невой,
Двѣнадцать мѣсяцевъ поютъ о смертномъ часѣ,
Струится въ воздухѣ ледъ блѣдно-голубой.

Декабрь торжественный струитъ свое дыханье,
Какъ будто въ комнатѣ тяжелая Нева.
Нѣтъ, не Соломинка, Лигейя, умиранье —
Я научился вамъ, блаженныя слова.

SOLOMINKA (THE STRAW) [6]

I

When you are not sleeping, Solominka,
In your enormous bedroom, and are waiting,
Dreamless, for the high and heavy ceiling to come down
With quiet sorrow on your keen eyes,

Sonorous Solomka, or seasoned Solominka,
You've drunk down all death, grown tender and
Been broken, my dear Solomka, no more alive—
Not Salome, no, it is Solominka.

In hours of sleeplessness, objects are heavier
As if fewer of them—such a stillness—
The cushions glitter in the mirror, grow almost white,
And the bed is reflected in the round pool.

No, it is not Solomka in her solemn silk
In a huge room above the black Neva.
For twelve months they sing of the final hour,
And the pale blue ice waves in the air.

Solemn December sends out its breath
As if the great Neva were in the room.
No, not Solominka—Ligeia, departed—
I have found you, glorious words.

II

Я научился вамъ, блаженныя слова,
Леноръ, Соломинка, Лигейя, Серафита,
Въ огромной комнатѣ тяжелая Нева,
И голубая кровь струится изъ гранита.

Декабрь торжественный сіяетъ надъ Невой.
Двѣнадцать мѣсяцевъ поютъ о смертномъ часѣ.
Нѣтъ, не соломинка въ торжественномъ атласѣ
Вкушаетъ медленный, томительный покой.

Въ моей крови живетъ декабрьская Лигейя,
Чья въ саркофагѣ спитъ блаженная любовь,
А та, соломинка, быть можетъ Саломея,
Убита жалостью и не вернется вновь.

1916

II

I have found you, blessed words:
—Lenore, Solominka, Ligeia, Seraphita—
In the enormous room, the great Neva,
And from the granite, the blue blood flows.

Solemn December shines above the Neva.
For twelve months they sing of the final hour.
No, not Solominka in her silks
Enjoying a slow, oppressive rest.

In my blood lives Decembrish Ligeia,
Whose blissful love sleeps in a sarcophagus,
But that *solominka*, perhaps Salome,
Was crushed with pity, and shall never return.

— Я потеряла нѣжную камею,
Не знаю гдѣ, на берегу Невы.
Я римлянку прелестную жалѣю —
Чуть не въ слезахъ мнѣ говорили вы.

Но для чего, прекрасная грузинка,
Тревожить прахъ божественныхъ гробницъ?
Еще одна пушистая снѣжинка
Растаяла на вѣерѣ рѣсницъ.

И кроткую вы наклонили шею.
Камеи нѣтъ — нѣтъ римлянки, увы.
Я Тинотину смуглую жалѣю —
Дѣвичій Римъ на берегу Невы.

1916

"I've lost a delicate cameo,
Somewhere on the Neva's shore.
I pity the beautiful Roman girl,"
You said to me, almost in tears.

But why, fair Georgian woman,
Stir up the dust on a sacred tomb?
Another downy snowflake
Melted on her eyelid's fan.

You bowed your gentle neck.
Alas, no cameo, no Roman girl.
I pity the tawny Tinotine—virgin
Rome on the Neva's shore.

Собирались эллины войною
На прелестный островъ Саламинъ.
Онъ, отторгнутъ вражеской рукою,
Виденъ былъ изъ гавани Аѳинъ.

А теперь друзья-островитяне
Снаряжаютъ наши корабли.
Не любили раньше англичане
Европейской сладостной земли.

О, Европа, новая Эллада,
Охраняй Акрополь и Пирей.
Намъ подарковъ съ острова не надо,
Цѣлый лѣсъ незваныхъ кораблей.

1916

The Greeks planned for war
On delightful Salamis [7].
From the harbor of Athens, you could see it
Held in the enemy's grip.

And now our friends the islanders
Are shelling our own ships.
Earlier the English failed to love
The sweet European soil.

O, Europe, new Hellas,
Save the Acropolis and Pireus.
We do not need the island's gifts,
A forest of uninvited ships.

I

Мнѣ холодно. Прозрачная весна
Въ зеленый пухъ Петрополь одѣваетъ
Но, какъ медуза, невская волна
Мнѣ отвращенье легкое внушаетъ.
По набережной сѣверной рѣки
Автомобилей мчатся свѣтляки,
Летятъ стрекозы и жуки стальные,
Мерцаютъ звѣздъ булавки золотыя,
Но никакія звѣзды не убьютъ
Морской воды тяжелый изумрудъ.

II

Въ Петрополѣ прозрачномъ мы умремъ,
Гдѣ властвуетъ надъ нами Прозерпина.
Мы въ каждомъ вздохѣ смертный воздухъ пьемъ,
И каждый часъ намъ смертная година.
Богиня моря, грозная Аѳина,
Сними могучій каменный шеломъ.
Въ Петрополѣ прозрачномъ мы умремъ,
Здѣсь царствуешь не ты, а Прозерпина.

1916

I

I am cold. Clear Spring dresses
Petropolis in verdant down.
But like a medusa [8], the Neva's wave
Stirs up in me a slight aversion.
Along the northern bank,
The headlights speed away.
Steel dragonflies and beetles are flying,
Golden pinpoints of starlight glimmer,
But not one of those stars surpasses
The massive emerald of the water's wave.

II

We shall die in transparent Petropolis
Where Persephone reigns over us.
We drink with every breath the deadly air
And every hour is our last.
Terrible Athena, goddess of the sea,
Remove your mighty helmet of stone.
We shall die in transparent Petropolis,
Where Persephone rules, not you.

1

Не вѣря воскресенья чуду,
На кладбищѣ гуляли мы.
— Ты знаешь, мнѣ земля повсюду
Напоминаетъ тѣ холмы

. . . .

. . . .

Гдѣ обрывается Россія
Надъ моремъ чернымъ и глухимъ.

2

Отъ монастырскихъ косогоровъ
Широкій убѣгаетъ лугъ.
Мнѣ отъ владимирскихъ просторовъ
Такъ не хотѣлося на югъ,
Но въ этой темной, деревянной
И юродивой слободѣ
Съ такой монашкою туманной
Остаться — значитъ быть бѣдѣ.

3

Цѣлую локоть загорѣлый
И лба кусочекъ восковой.
Я знаю — онъ остался бѣлый
Подъ смуглой прядью золотой.
Цѣлую кисть, гдѣ отъ браслета
Еще бѣлѣетъ полоса.
Тавриды пламенное лѣто
Творитъ такія чудеса.

4

Какъ скоро ты смуглянкой стала
И къ Спасу бѣдному пришла,
Не отрываясь цѣловала,
А гордою въ Москвѣ была.
Намъ остается только имя:
Чудесный звукъ, на долгій срокъ.
Прими жъ ладонями моими
Пересыпаемый песокъ.

1916

1

Not believing in the Resurrection,
we strolled to the cemetery.
"You know, the earth everywhere
reminds me of those hills

·   ·   ·   ·   ·   ·   ·

·   ·   ·   ·   ·   ·   ·

where Russia breaks off
above the black, deaf sea.

2

The broad meadow runs away
from the monastery's slopes.
I didn't really want to be
south of Vladimir's expanse,
but to stay in this wooded, dark,
and crazy place with such a dizzy nun
means to be in misery.

3

I kiss the sunburned elbow
and a waxen patch of forehead.
I know it is still white
under the tawny golden locks.
I kiss the wrist where a bracelet
has left a white band.
The flaming summer of the Taurides [9]
causes such marvels.

4

How quickly you browned,
and approached the poor Savior,
embraced Him, unrebuked —
but in Moscow, you were proud.
Only the name is left for us —
a marvelous sound for a long time.
Take this sand being poured
with my hands.

Эта ночь непоправима,
А у васъ еще свѣтло.
У воротъ Ерусалима
Солнце черное взошло.

Солнце желтое страшнѣе.
Баю, баюшки, баю,
Въ свѣтломъ храмѣ Iудеи
Хоронили мать мою.

Благодати не имѣя
И священства лишены,
Въ свѣтломъ храмѣ Iудеи
Отпѣвали прахъ жены.

И надъ матерью звенѣли
Голоса израильтянъ.
— Я проснулся въ колыбели,
Чернымъ солнцемъ осіянъ

1916

This night is beyond recall,
But your house is still bright.
At the gates of Jerusalem,
The black sun has risen.

The yellow sun is more fearful—
Baiu, baiushki, baiu... [10]
In a bright temple, the Jews
Have hidden my mother.

Not having Grace,
Deprived of priesthood,
The Jews, in a bright temple,
Chanted ovder the woman's dust.

And the voices of the Israelites
Rose above the mother.
I awoke in a cradle, shone upon
By a black sun.

ДЕКАБРИСТЪ

„Тому свидѣтельство языческій сенатъ —
Сіи дѣла не умираютъ.“
Онъ раскурилъ чубукъ и запахнулъ халатъ,
А рядомъ въ шахматы играютъ.

Честолюбивый сонъ онъ промѣнялъ на срубъ
Въ глухомъ урочищѣ Сибири
И вычурный чубукъ у ядовитыхъ губъ,
Сказавшихъ правду въ скорбномъ мірѣ.

Шумѣли въ первый разъ германскіе дубы,
Европа плакала въ тенетахъ,
Квадриги черныя вставали на дыбы
На тріумфальныхъ поворотахъ.

Бывало, голубой въ стаканахъ пуншъ горитъ,
Съ широкимъ шумомъ самовара
Подруга рейнская тихонько говоритъ,
Вольнолюбивая гитара.

Еще волнуются живые голоса
О сладкой вольности гражданства,
Но жертвы не хотятъ слѣпыя небеса,
Вѣрнѣе трудъ и постоянство.

Все перепуталось, и некому сказать,
Что, постепенно холодѣя,
Все перепуталось, и сладко повторять:
Россія, Лета, Лорелея.

1917

THE DECEMBRIST

" To this the pagan senate testifies:
—THESE DEEDS SHALL NEVER DIE!—"
He lit his pipe and wrapped his cloak around
While some play chess nearby.

He bartered his ambitious dream
For a godforsaken Siberian plot
And an elegant pipe at the venomous lips
Which uttered truth in a tortured world.

When the German oaks first rustled,
Europe wept in their shade.
Black horses in *quadrigae* [11] reared
on each triumphant turn.

Once, the azure punch glowed in our glasses.
With the broad noises of the samovar,
A friend from across the Rhine spoke
In muted tones, a freedom-loving guitar.

The lively voices murmur still
About the sweet liberty of citizenship;
But the martyrs don't want blind skies,
Toil and Consistency are truer.

Everything's confused and there is no one to say,
As things grow colder,
Everything's confused, nor sweetly repeat:
Russia, Lethe, Lorelei...

МЕГАНОМЪ.

1

Еще далеко асфоделей
Прозрачно-сѣрая весна,
Пока еще на самомъ дѣлѣ
Шуршитъ песокъ, кипитъ волна.
Но здѣсь душа моя вступаетъ,
Какъ Персефона въ легкій кругъ,
И въ царствѣ мертвыхъ не бываетъ
Прелестныхъ загорѣлыхъ рукъ.

2

Зачѣмъ же лодкѣ довѣряемъ
Мы тяжесть урны гробовой
И праздникъ черныхъ розъ свершаемъ
Надъ аметистовой водой?
Туда душа моя стремится,
За мысъ туманный Меганомъ,
И черный парусъ возвратится
Оттуда послѣ похоронъ.

3

Какъ быстро тучи пробѣгаютъ
Неосвѣщенною грядой,
И хлопья черныхъ розъ летаютъ
Подъ этой вѣтреной луной,
И, птица смерти и рыданья,
Влачится траурной каймой
Огромный флагъ воспоминанья
За кипарисною кормой.

4

И раскрывается съ шуршаньемъ
Печальный вѣеръ прошлыхъ лѣтъ
Туда, гдѣ съ темнымъ содроганьемъ
Въ песку зарылся амулетъ.
Туда душа моя стремится,
За мысъ туманный Меганомъ,
И черный парусъ возвратится
Оттуда послѣ похоронъ.

MEGANOM'

1

Still far the asphodels,
grey-transparent Spring.
Meanwhile, the sand rustles,
the wave foams.
But here, like Persephone,
my soul joins the gentle circle,
and in the realm of the dead,
seductive, sunburnt arms
do not exist.

2

Why do we trust the boat
with the heaviness of the funerary urn,
and end the festival of black roses
over amethystine water?
My soul rushes there,
to the cloudy cape of Meganom',
and from there the black sail will return
after the funeral.

3

How quickly clouds pass
in a sunless row and
petals of black roses drift
under this windy moon.
There is a bird of death and weeping,
and the enormous flag of remembrance
is dragged along the mournful border
behind a cypress stern.

4

The sorrowful fan of past years
unfolds with a riffle.
My soul rushes there,
to the cloudy cape of Meganom',
where with dark trembling, an amulet
is buried in the sand, and from there
after the funeral
the black sail returns.

Когда на площадяхъ и въ тишинѣ келейной
Мы сходимъ медленно съ ума,
Холоднаго и чистаго рейнвейна
Предложитъ намъ жестокая зима.

Въ серебряномъ ведрѣ намъ предлагаетъ стужа
Валгаллы бѣлое вино,
И свѣтлый образъ сѣвернаго мужа
Напоминаетъ намъ оно.

Но сѣверные скальды грубы,
Не знаютъ радостей игры,
И сѣвернымъ дружинамъ любы
Янтарь, пожары и пиры.

Имъ только снится воздухъ юга,
Чужого неба волшебство.
— И все таки упрямая подруга
Откажется попробовать его.

1917

When on the squares and in private silence
We slowly go out of our minds,
Brutal winter will toast us
With cold and clear Rhine wine.

The frost offers us in a silver pail
The white wine of Valhalla,
And for us it recalls
A clear picture of a northern man.

But northern skalds are rude,
Don't know the joy of the game,
The only loves of northern troops
Are amber, feasts and flames.

They dream only of the southern air,
The magic of a foreign sky—
Nevertheless the stubborn friend
Still refuses to try.

Среди священниковъ левитомъ молодымъ
На стражѣ утренней онъ долго оставался.
Ночь іудейская сгущалася надъ нимъ,
И храмъ разрушенный угрюмо созидался.

Онъ говорилъ: Небесъ тревожна желтизна,
Ужъ надъ Евфратомъ ночь, бѣгите, іереи.
А старцы думали: Не наша въ томъ вина.
Се черно-желтый свѣтъ, се радость Іудеи.

Онъ съ нами былъ, когда на берегу ручья
Мы въ драгоцѣнный ленъ субботу пеленали
И семисвѣщникомъ тяжелымъ освѣщали
Іерусалима ночь и чадъ небытія.

1917

The young Levite among the priests
Stayed long on morning vigil.
Jewish night grew thick around him,
And the ruined temple was solemnly raised.

He said: the yellowing of the skies is alarming.
Run, priests, for night is already over the Euphrates!
But the elders thought: this is not our fault;
Behold the black and yellow light, the joy of the Jews.

He was with us when, on the river's shore,
We swaddled the Sabbath in precious linen
With a heavy Menorah lit the night of Jerusalem,
The smoke of non-existence.

1

Золотистаго меду струя изъ бутылки текла
Такъ тягуче и долго, что молвить хозяйка успѣла:
Здѣсь, въ печальной Тавридѣ, куда насъ судьба занесла,
Мы совсѣмъ не скучаемъ — и черезъ плечо поглядѣла.

2

Всюду Бахуса службы, какъ будто на свѣтѣ одни
Сторожа и собаки. Идешь — никого не замѣтишь.
Какъ тяжелыя бочки, спокойные катятся дни,
Далеко въ шалашѣ голоса: не поймешь, не отвѣтишь.

3

Послѣ чаю мы вышли въ огромный, коричневый садъ,
Какъ рѣсницы, на окнахъ опущены темныя шторы,
Мимо бѣлыхъ колоннъ мы пошли посмотрѣть виноградъ,
Гдѣ воздушнымъ стекломъ обливаются сонныя горы.

4

Я сказалъ: виноградъ какъ старинная битва живетъ,
Гдѣ курчавые всадники бьются въ кудрявомъ порядкѣ.
Въ каменистой Тавридѣ наука Эллады — и вотъ
Золотыхъ десятинъ благородныя ржавыя грядки.

5

Ну, а въ комнатѣ бѣлой, какъ прялка, стоитъ тишина,
Пахнетъ уксусомъ, краской и свѣжимъ виномъ
                                        изъ подвала.
Помнишь, въ греческомъ домѣ любимая всѣми жена,
Не Елена — другая — какъ долго она вышивала.

6

Золотое руно, гдѣ же ты, золотое руно —
Всю дорогу шумѣли морскія тяжелыя волны,
И, покинувъ корабль, натрудившій въ моряхъ полотно,
Одиссей возвратился, пространствомъ и временемъ
                                        полный.

1917

34

1

The thick golden stream of honey took so long
To pour, our host had time to say:
"Here in the dismal Taurides, where fate has brought us,
We don't get bored at all"—and she looked over her shoulder.

2

The services of Bacchus everywhere, as if on earth
Were only guards and dogs. You go along, you notice no one—
Like heavy barrels, the peaceful days roll by:
Far off. Voices in a hut: you do not apprehend, nor reply.

3

After tea, we went out in the huge brown garden,
The dark blinds were lowered like eyelashes.
Past white columns, we strolled to the vineyard,
Where the drowsy mountains are glazed with airy glass.

4

I said: a vineyard is like an ancient battle
Where curly-headed horsemen fight in twisted order.
Hellenic science in the stony Taurides—and here
There are the noble, rusty layers of golden acres.

5

Silence stands like a spinning wheel in the white room.
From the cellar, smells of paint, vinegar, fresh wine.
Do you recall, in the Greek house: the woman courted
By everyone—not Helen—another—how long she wove?

6

Golden fleece, where are you, golden fleece?
The sea's heavy waves roared the whole way.
Abandoning the ship, its sail worn out,
Odysseus returned, full with space and time.

Въ тотъ вечеръ не гудѣлъ стрѣльчатый лѣсъ органа.
Намъ пѣла Шуберта родная колыбель,
Шумѣла мельница, и въ пѣсняхъ урагана
Смѣялся музыки голубоглазый хмель.

Старинной пѣсни міръ коричневый, зеленый,
Но только вѣчно-молодой,
Гдѣ соловьиныхъ липъ рокочущія кроны
Съ звѣриной яростью качаетъ царь лѣсной.

И сила страшная ночного возвращенья,
Та пѣсня дикая, какъ черное вино.
Это двойникъ — пустое привидѣнье
Безсмысленно глядитъ въ холодное окно.

1918

That evening the forest of organ pipes did not resound.
Schubert was sung for us—a native lullaby.
The mill was grinding, the music's blue-eyed drunkenness
Laughed in the songs of the hurricane.

The world of old song is brown, green,
But only eternally young where the Forest-king
Shakes the rumbling crowns of nightingaled
Linden trees in senseless rage.

The awesome strength of night's return
Is that wild song, like black wine:
It is a double, a hollow ghost
Peering absurdly through the cold window!

Твое чудесное произношенье,
Горячій посвистъ хищныхъ птицъ,
Скажу ль — живое впечатлѣнье
Какихъ то шелковыхъ рѣсницъ.

„Что“ — Голова отяжелѣла...
„Во“ — Это я тебя зову.
И далеко прошелестѣло:
Я тоже на землѣ живу.

Пусть говорятъ: любовь крылата.
Смерть окрыленнѣе стократъ.
Еще душа борьбой объята,
А наши губы къ ней летятъ.

И столько воздуха, и шелка,
И вѣтра въ шопотѣ твоемъ,
И, какъ слѣпые, ночью долгой
Мы смѣсь безсолнечную пьемъ,

1918

Your marvelous pronunciation—
The parched whistle of birds of prey;
Or should I say: a living impression
Of some silken summer lightning.

What?—your head grew heavy.
Was? [12]—I am calling you.
And far away, a whisper:
I, too, live on earth.

Let them talk: love has wings,
Death, a hundred more;
My soul is filled with strife,
But our lips fly to it.

So much air and silk and
Wind in your whisper,
Like blind men, the long night
We drink a sunless mixture.

TRISTIA

1

Я изучилъ науку разставанья
Въ простоволосыхъ жалобахъ ночныхъ.
Жуютъ волы, и длится ожиданье,
Послѣдній часъ веселій городскихъ,
И чту обрядъ той пѣтушиной ночи,
Когда, поднявъ дорожной скорби грузъ,
Глядѣли въ даль заплаканныя очи,
И женскій плачъ мѣшался съ пѣньемъ музъ.

2

Кто можетъ знать при словѣ — разставанье,
Какая намъ разлука предстоитъ,
Что намъ сулитъ пѣтушье восклицанье,
Когда огонь въ Акрополѣ горитъ,
И на зарѣ какой то новой жизни,
Когда въ сѣняхъ лѣниво волъ жуетъ,
Зачѣмъ пѣтухъ, глашатай новой жизни,
На городской стѣнѣ крылами бьетъ?

3

И я люблю обыкновенье пряжи,
Снуетъ челнокъ, веретено жужжитъ.
Смотри, навстрѣчу, словно пухъ лебяжій,
Уже босая Делія летитъ.
О, нашей жизни скудная основа,
Куда какъ бѣденъ радости языкъ!
Все было встарь, все повторится снова,
И сладокъ намъ лишь узнаванья мигъ.

4

Да будетъ такъ: прозрачная фигурка
На чистомъ блюдѣ глиняномъ лежитъ,
Какъ бѣличья распластанная шкурка,
Склонясь надъ воскомъ, дѣвушка глядитъ.
Не намъ гадать о греческомъ Эребѣ,
Для женщинъ воскъ, что для мужчины медъ.
Намъ только въ битвахъ выпадаетъ жребій,
А имъ дано гадая умереть.

1918

TRISTIA

1

I've learned the science of parting
In the laments of night, her hair let down.
Oxen graze, and the waiting's drawn out.
The town's last hour of vigil, and I
Revere the ritual of the night when
The cock crowed and exhausted eyes
Raised their load of wandering sorrow,
Gazed into the distance, and a woman's weep
And muse's song combined.

2

Who knows, at the mention of "farewell,"
What separation awaits us,
What the cockscrow augurs
When flames glow in the acropolis,
And on the dawn of some new life,
While an ox chews lazily in his shed,
Why the cock, herald of new life,
Beats his wings on the town's walls?

3

And I love the practice of spinning:
Shuttle weaves, spindle buzzes,
Look how barefoot Delia flies
To meet you, like swansdown.
Oh, the meager warp of our life,
Like the thin language of joy!
All things were in ancient times,
All will be again and only the instant
Of recognition is sweet to us.

4

So be it: a transparent figure
Lies on a clean earthen dish,
Like the spread pelt of a squirrel,
And the girl stares, bowing over the wax. [13]
We cannot tell the fortunes of Grecian Erebus,
Wax is for women what bronze is for men.
Our fate slips out only in battle,
But they die telling fortunes.

ЧЕРЕПАХА

1

На каменныхъ отрогахъ Піэріи
Водили музы первый хороводъ,
Чтобы, какъ пчелы, лирники слѣпые
Намъ подарили іонійскій медъ.
И холодкомъ повѣяло высокимъ
Отъ выпукло-дѣвическаго лба,
Чтобы раскрылись правнукамъ далекимъ
Архипелага нѣжные гроба.

2

Бѣжитъ весна топтать луга Эллады,
Обула Сафо пестрый сапожекъ,
И молоточками куютъ цикады,
Какъ въ пѣсенкѣ поется перстенекъ.
Высокій домъ построилъ плотникъ дюжій,
На свадьбу всѣхъ передушили куръ,
И растянулъ сапожникъ неуклюжій
На башмаки всѣ пять воловьихъ шкуръ.

3

Нерасторопна черепаха-лира,
Едва-едва безпалая ползетъ,
Лежитъ себѣ на солнышкѣ Эпира,
Тихонько грѣя золотой животъ.
Ну, кто ее такую приласкаетъ,
Кто спящую ее перевернетъ?
Она во снѣ Терпандра ожидаетъ,
Сухихъ перстовъ предчувствуя налетъ.

4

Поитъ дубы холодная криница,
Простоволосая шумитъ трава,
На радость осамъ пахнетъ медуница.
О, гдѣ же вы, святые острова,
Гдѣ не ѣдятъ надломленнаго хлѣба,
Гдѣ только медъ, вино и молоко,
Скрипучій трудъ не омрачаетъ неба,
И колесо вращается легко.

1919

TORTOISE

1

On the stony spurs of Pierius [14]
The Muses conducted the first chorus
So blind lyrists, like bees, might give us
Ionic honey.
With a great chill, it began to blow
From the virgin's prominent forehead
So the tender graves of the Archipelago
Might be uncovered for distant grandsons.

2

Spring rushes to trample the meadows of Hellas,
Sappho puts on a dappled boot,
Cicadas click like hammers forging out a ring,
As in the little song. [15]
A stout carpenter built a tall house,
They strangled all the hens at a wedding,
An inept cobbler stretched
All five ox-hides for shoes.

3

The slow lyre-tortoise
Barely creeps along,
Sets herself down in the sun of Epirus, [16]
Quietly warming her golden belly.
Who will caress her so,
Who will turn her over, sleeping—
She awaits Terpander in her sleep,
Foreseeing the sudden sweep of dry fingers.

4

A cold sprinkle waters the oaks,
The untrimmed grasses murmur,
The honeysuckle smells, to the joy of the bees.
O where are you, sacred islands,
Where they do not eat broken bread,
Where there is only wine, milk and honey,
Creaking toil does not darken the sky, and
The wheel turns easily.

Идемъ туда, гдѣ разныя науки
И ремесло — шашлыкъ и чебуреки,
Гдѣ вывѣска, изображая брюки,
Даетъ понятье намъ о человѣкѣ.
Мужской сюртукъ — безъ головы стремленье,
Цирюльника летающая скрипка
И месмерическій утюгъ — явленье
Небесныхъ прачекъ — тяжести улыбка...

Здѣсь дѣвушки старѣющія въ челкахъ
Обдумываютъ странные наряды,
И адмиралы въ твердыхъ треуголкахъ
Припоминаютъ сонъ Шехеразады.
Прозрачна даль. Немного винограда,
И неизмѣнно дуетъ вѣтеръ свѣжій.
Недалеко отъ Смирны и Богдада,
Но трудно плыть, а звѣзды всюду тѣ же.

1919

1

Let us go where there are varied crafts
And trades—*shashlik* and *chebureki*,
Where trousers on a sign give us
The idea of a man.
A man's frock coat: desire without a head.
The barber's flying fiddle, a mesmerizing iron,
The appearance of heavenly washer-women—
The smile of heaviness.

2

Here, the girls, greying in the forelocks,
Contemplate the strange dresses,
Admirals in stiff three-cornered hats
Bring Scheherezade's dream to mind.
The distance is clear. A few vineyards.
Always a fresh wind blowing.
Not far from Smyrna and Baghdad,
But difficult to navigate,
For the stars are everywhere the same. [17]

1

Въ хрустальномъ омутѣ какая крутизна!
За насъ сіенскіе предстательствуютъ горы,
И сумасшедшихъ скалъ колючіе соборы
Повисли въ воздухѣ, гдѣ шерсть и тишина.

2

Съ висячей лѣстницы пророковъ и царей
Спускается органъ, святого духа крѣпость,
Овчарокъ бодрый лай и добрая свирѣпость,
Овчины пастуховъ и посохи судей.

3

Вотъ неподвижная земля, и вмѣстѣ съ ней
Я христіанства пью холодный горный воздухъ,
Крутое Вѣрую и псалмопѣвца роздыхъ,
Ключи и рубища апостольскихъ церквей.

4

Какая линія могла бы передать
Хрусталь высокихъ нотъ въ эфирѣ укрѣпленномъ,
И съ христіанскихъ горъ въ пространствѣ изумленномъ,
Какъ Палестины пѣснь, нисходитъ благодать.

1919

1

In a crystal pool, such steepness!
Behind us, the sienna mountains protect,
Jagged cathedrals of raving mad cliffs
Are suspended in the air,
Where there is wool and silence.

2

From the hanging staircase of prophets and kings,
Descends an organ, the fortress of the Holy Ghost,
The brave barking and gentle ferocity of sheepdogs,
The sheepskins of shepherds, and the staffs of judges.

3

Here is unmovable ground, and along with it
I drink the cold mountain air of Christianity,
The stern Credo and the psalmist's lull,
The keys and tatters of apostolic churches.

4

That such a line could deliver
Crystal high notes in the invigorating ether,
And from the Christian mountains in the astounding space,
A blessing descends, like a song of Palestine.

Природа тотъ же Римъ, и отразилась въ немъ.
Мы видимъ образы его гражданской мощи
Въ прозрачномъ воздухѣ, какъ въ циркѣ голубомъ,
На форумѣ полей и въ колоннадѣ рощи.

Природа тотъ же Римъ, и кажется опять
Намъ незачѣмъ боговъ напрасно безпокоить,
Есть внутренности жертвъ, чтобъ о войнѣ гадать,
Рабы, чтобы молчать, и камни, чтобы строить.

Nature's the same as Rome, was reflected in it.
We see images of its civic might
In the clear air, as in the sky-blue circus,
In the forum of fields, the colonnades of groves.

Nature is the same as Rome, again it seems
We needn't trouble God in vain.
We've got the viscera of the sacrifice
To tell the fortunes of war, and slaves
To keep the silence, and stones with which to build.

Только дѣтскія книги читать,
Только дѣтскія думы лелѣять,
Все большое далеко развѣять,
Изъ глубокой печали возстать.

Я отъ жизни смертельно усталъ,
Ничего отъ нея не пріемлю,
Но люблю мою бѣдную землю,
Оттого что иной не видалъ.

Я качался въ далекомъ саду
На простой деревянной качели,
И высокія темныя ели
Вспоминаю въ туманномъ бреду.

To read only children's books,
To have only childish thoughts,
To throw away everything grown-up,
To rise from deep sadness.

I am deathly tired of life,
I will accept nothing from it.
But I love my poor earth,
For I have seen no other.

I rocked in a distant garden
On a plain wooden swing,
Tall dark fir trees
I recall in a feverish haze.

Вернись въ смѣсительное лоно,
Откуда, Лія, ты пришла,
За то, что солнцу Илліона
Ты желтый сумракъ предпочла.

Иди, никто тебя не тронетъ,
На грудь отца, въ глухую ночь,
Пускай главу свою уронитъ
Кровосмѣсительница — дочь.

Но роковая перемѣна
Въ тебѣ исполниться должна.
Ты будешь Лія — не Елена.
Не потому наречена,

Что царской крови тяжелѣе
Струится въ жилахъ, чѣмъ другой —
Нѣтъ, ты полюбишь іудея,
Исчезнешь въ немъ — и Богъ съ тобой.

Go back to the tainted lap, Leah,
Whence you came,
You preferred yellow twilight
To the sun of Ilion.

Go, no one will touch you,
Let the incestuous daughter
Drop her head on her father's breast
In the dead of night.

But the fatal change
Must be fulfilled in you;
You shall be Leah—not Helen—
Thus not chosen,

For it is harder for royal blood
To flow in the veins—
No, you are in love with a Jew,
You will vanish in him, and
God will be with you.

О, этотъ воздухъ, смутой пьяный,
На черной площади Кремля
Качаютъ шаткій „миръ" смутьяны,
Тревожно пахнутъ тополя.

Соборовъ восковые лики,
Колоколовъ дремучій лѣсъ,
Какъ бы разбойникъ безъязыкій
Въ стропилахъ каменныхъ исчезъ.

А въ запечатанныхъ соборахъ,
Гдѣ и прохладно, и темно,
Какъ въ нѣжныхъ глиняныхъ амфорахъ,
Играетъ русское вино.

Успенскій, дивно округленный,
Весь удивленье райскихъ дугъ,
И Благовѣщенскій, зеленый,
И, мнится, заворкуетъ вдругъ.

Архангельскій и Воскресенья
Просвѣчиваютъ, какъ ладонь —
Повсюду скрытое горѣнье,
Въ кувшинахъ спрятанный огонь...

O this air, intoxicated with unrest,
On the black square of the Kremlin.
The agitators rock the teetering world. [18]
Restlessly the poplars sway.

The waxen facades of the cathedrals,
The thick forest of bells,
As if a tongueless bandit
Had vanished in the stony rafters.

But in the sealed cathedrals,
Where it is cool and dark,
Like delicate clay amphoras,
The Russian wine plays.

The Assumption, surprisingly rotund,
All the marvel of the arches of Paradise,
And the Annunciation in green,
Begins suddenly to crow.

The Archangel and Resurrection [19]
Shine like sheets of glass,
Everywhere the secret burning,—
In the wine jugs a hidden flame...

1

Въ Петербургѣ мы сойдемся снова,
Словно солнце мы похоронили въ немъ,
И блаженное, безсмысленное слово
Въ первый разъ произнесемъ.
Въ черномъ бархатѣ совѣтской ночи,
Въ бархатѣ всемірной пустоты,
Все поютъ блаженныхъ женъ родныя очи,
Все цвѣтутъ безсмертныя цвѣты.

2

Дикой кошкой горбится столица,
На мосту патруль стоитъ,
Только злой моторъ во мглѣ промчится
И кукушкой прокричитъ.
Мнѣ не надо пропуска ночного,
Часовыхъ я не боюсь:
За блаженное, безсмысленное слово
Я въ ночи совѣтской помолюсь.

3

Слышу легкій театральный шорохъ
И дѣвическое „ахъ“ —
И безсмертныхъ розъ огромный ворохъ
У Киприды на рукахъ.
У костра мы грѣемся отъ скуки,
Можетъ быть вѣка пройдутъ,
И блаженныхъ женъ родныя руки
Легкій пепелъ соберутъ.

4

Гдѣ то грядки красныя партера,
Пышно взбиты шифоньерки ложъ;
Заводная кукла офицера;
Не для черныхъ душъ и низменныхъ святошъ...
Что жъ, гаси, пожалуй, наши свѣчи
Въ черномъ бархатѣ всемірной пустоты,
Все поютъ блаженныхъ женъ крутыя плечи,
А ночного солнца не замѣтишь ты.

25 Ноября 1920 г.

1

In Petersburg we'll meet again,
As though we'd buried the sun there,
And for the first time utter
The blessed, senseless word.
In the black velvet of Soviet night,
In the velvet of world-wide emptiness,
The kind eyes of blessed women still sing,
The immortal flowers still bloom.

2

The capitol arches like a savage cat,
A patrol is standing on the bridge,
A single angry car speeds by in the dark,
And cries out like a cuckoo.
This evening I do not need a pass,
I am not afraid of the sentries:
I will pray in the Soviet night
For the blessed and senseless word.

3

I hear a light rustling in the theater
And a young girl's "Oh" —
In Kypris' [20] arms, a huge bunch
Of immortal roses.
Out of boredom, we warm ourselves
By a bonfire. Perhaps centuries will pass,
And the kind hands of blessed women
Will gather up the light ashes.

4

Somewhere the red rows of the gallery,
The sumptuous chiffon of the boxes;
The clockwork-puppet officer;
Not for black souls or vile hypocrites...
Yes. Extinguish, please, our tapers
In the black velvet of world-wide emptiness,
The sloped shoulders of blessed women still sing,
But you don't notice the night sun.

На перламутровый челнокъ
Натягивая шелка нити,
О, пальцы гибкіе, начните
Очаровательный урокъ.

Приливы и отливы рукъ,
Однобразныя движенья,
Ты заклинаешь, безъ сомнѣнья,
Какой то солнечный испугъ,

Когда широкая ладонь,
Какъ раковина, пламенѣя,
То гаснетъ, къ тѣнямъ тяготѣя,
То въ розовый уйдетъ огонь.

Stretching taut the silken threads
On a mother-of-pearl shuttle,
O, lithe fingers, begin
Your fascinating lesson.

Ebb and flow of your hands,
Monotonous movements,
No doubt you are conjuring
Some kind of solar fright,

When your broad palm,
Like a shell, a flame,
First dies down, drawn to the shadows,
Then sinks at last in a rosy light.

Отъ легкой жизни мы сошли съ ума.
Съ утра вино, а съ вечера похмелье.
Какъ удержать напрасное веселье,
Румянецъ твой, о пьяная чума?

Въ пожатьи рукъ мучительный обрядъ,
На улицахъ ночные поцѣлуи,
Когда рѣчныя тяжелѣютъ струи,
И фонари, какъ факелы, горятъ.

Мы смерти ждемъ, какъ сказочнаго волка,
Но я боюсь, что раньше всѣхъ умретъ
Тотъ, у кого тревожно-красный ротъ
И на глаза спадающая челка.

Out of our minds with the easy life,
Wine from morning on, hungover by evening,
How can I retain this idle gaiety,
Your blush, O drunken plague.

An agonizing ceremony in a handshake,
Nocturnal kisses on the streets,
The flow of speech grows heavy,
Lanterns burn like torches.

We wait for death, like the fairytale wolf.
But I'm afraid that before everyone else,
Will die the one with the anxious red mouth
And the forelock over his eyes.

Что поютъ часы-кузнечикъ,
Лихорадка шелеститъ,
И шуршитъ сухая печка, —
Это красный шелкъ горитъ.

Что зубами мыши точатъ
Жизни тоненькое дно,
Это ласточка и дочкѣ
Отвязала мой челнокъ.

Что на крышѣ дождь бормочетъ, —
Это черный шелкъ горитъ,
Но черемуха услышитъ
И на днѣ морскомъ проститъ.

Потому что смерть невинныхъ,
И ничѣмъ нельзя помочь,
Что въ горячкѣ соловьиной
Сердце теплое еще.

The clockhoppers sing,
and fever whispers
and dry stove crackles:
It is red silk burning.

The mice grind with their teeth
the very thin ground of life—
a swallow and her daughter
have loosened my shuttle.

Rain murmurs on the roof—
It is black silk burning,
but the bird cherry will hear,
and on the bottom of the sea: forgive.

Because death is guiltless, and
there is no cure for anything,
in a nightingale's fever,
there is still a warm heart.

Уничтожаетъ пламень
Сухую жизнь мою,
И нынѣ я не камень,
А дерево пою.

Оно легко и грубо;
Изъ одного куска
И сердцевина дуба,
И весла рыбака.

Вбивайте крѣпче сваи,
Стучите, молотки,
О деревянномъ раѣ,
Гдѣ вещи такъ легки.

The flame annihilates
My withered life,
Now it isn't stone
I sing, but wood.

It is light and rough;
Of a single slab
From the heart of the oak
The oars of the fisherman come.

Drive the pilings tighter.
Pound, you hammers,
Around the wooden paradise
Where things are so much easier.

Мнѣ Тифлисъ горбатый снится,
Сазандарій стонъ звенитъ,
На мосту народъ толпится,
Вся ковровая столица,
А внизу Кура шумитъ.

Надъ Курою есть духаны,
Гдѣ вино и милый пловъ,
И духанщикъ тамъ румяный
Подаетъ гостямъ стаканы
И служить тебѣ готовъ.

Кахетинское густое
Хорошо въ подвалѣ пить,
Тамъ въ прохладѣ, тамъ въ покоѣ
Пейте вдоволь, пейте двое:
Одному не надо пить.

Въ самомъ маленькомъ духанѣ
Ты товарища найдешь,
Если спросишь Теліани.
Поплыветъ Тифлисъ въ туманѣ,
Ты въ духанѣ поплывешь.

I dream of hunchbacked Tiflis,
Where a *Sazandar's* [21] groan resounds
The people cluster on the bridge,
The whole capital is carpeted,
And below, the Kura [22] murmurs.

Above the Kura are *dukhans* [23]
With their wine and good pilaf,
A ruddy *dukhanshchik*
Gives glasses to the guests,
He is ready to serve you.

The thick Cahetian wine
In the cellar is ready to drink—
There in the coolness, in peace,
You drink your fill, drink two,
Or you don't have to drink at all.

In the same, small *dukhan,*
If you ask for Teliani,
You will find a friend.
Tiflis is swimming in a fog,
Your head is swimming at the inn. [24]

Американка въ двадцать лѣтъ
Должна добраться до Египта,
Забывъ Титаника совѣтъ,
Что спитъ на днѣ мрачнѣе крипта.

Въ Америкѣ гудки поютъ,
И красныхъ небоскребовъ трубы
Холоднымъ тучамъ отдаютъ
Свои прокопченныя губы.

И въ Луврѣ океана дочь
Стоитъ, прекрасная, какъ тополь,
Чтобъ мраморъ сахарный толочь,
Влѣзаетъ бѣлкой на Акрополь.

Не понимая ничего,
Читаетъ Фауста въ вагонѣ
И сожалѣетъ, отчего
Людовик больше не на тронѣ.

An American girl of twenty
Has to get to Egypt,
Forgetting that Titanic advice
The bottom is darker than the crypt.

In America the sirens sing,
Red smokestack skyscrapers
Produce cold clouds
With their sooty lips.

In the Louvre is the ocean's
Daughter, beautiful as a poplar,
To crush the sugary marble
Climbs like a squirrel on the Acropolis.

She reads Faust in the carriage,
Understanding not a word,
And regrets that Louis
No longer holds the throne.

Сестры-тяжесть и нѣжность, одинаковы ваши примѣты,
Медуницы и осы тяжелую розу сосутъ,
Человѣкъ умираетъ, песокъ остываетъ согрѣтый,
И вчерашнее солнце на черныхъ носилкахъ несутъ.

Ахъ, тяжелыя соты и нѣжныя сѣти,
Легче камень поднять, чѣмъ вымолвить слово—любить,
У меня остается одна забота на свѣтѣ,
Золотая забота, какъ времени бремя избыть.

Словно темную воду, я пью помутившійся воздухъ,
Время вспахано плугомъ, и роза землею была,
Въ медленномъ водоворотѣ тяжелыя нѣжныя розы,
Розы тяжесть и нѣжность въ двойные вѣнки заплела.

    1920

Sisters—Heaviness, Tenderness—your signs are identical.
Bees and wasps suck the heavy rose.
A man dies, the heated sand grows cool, and
Yesterday's sun is carried away on a black stretcher.

Oh, heavy honeycombs, tender nets,
Easier to raise a stone than say your name!
I have one concern left on earth,
A golden one: to throw off time's yoke.

I drink the turbid air as if it were muddy water.
Time is ploughed up, and the rose was the earth.
In a slow vortex, love has twined the heavy,
Tender roses, the roses Heaviness and Tenderness,
Into double wreaths.

1

Я наравнѣ съ другими
Хочу тебѣ служить,
Отъ ревности сухими
Губами ворожить.
Не утоляетъ слово
Мнѣ пересохшихъ устъ,
И безъ тебя мнѣ снова
Дремучій воздухъ пустъ.

2

Я больше не ревную,
Но я тебя хочу,
И самъ себя несу я,
Какъ жертву, палачу.
Тебя не назову я
Ни радость, ни любовь;
На дикую, чужую,
Мнѣ подмѣнили кровь.

3

Еще одно мгновенье,
И я скажу тебѣ:
Не радость, а мученье
Я нахожу в тебѣ.
И, словно преступленье,
Меня къ тебѣ влечетъ
Искусанный, въ смятеньи,
Вишневый нѣжный ротъ.

4

Вернись ко мнѣ скорѣе:
Мнѣ страшно безъ тебя.
Я никогда сильнѣе
Не чувствовалъ тебя.
И въ полунощной драмѣ,
Во снѣ иль на яву,
Въ тревогѣ иль въ истомѣ —
Но я тебя зову.

1920

1

I want to serve you
On an equal footing with others;
From jealousy, to tell your fortune
With dry lips.
The word does not slake
My parched mouth,
And without you, again
The dense air is empty.

2

I am not jealous anymore,
But I want you,
And will suffer by myself
Like a hangman's victim.
I will call you
Neither joy, nor love;
Something wild and strange
Was substituted for my blood.

3

One more moment,
And I will say to you:
It is not joy, but torment
I find in you.
And, like some transgression,
It drags me to you,
The bitten, confused,
Tender cherry mouth.

4

Return to me sooner:
It is awful without you,
I have never felt
More strongly about you.
And in the midnight drama
In dream or reality,
Alarm or languor,
I shall call you.

1

Чуть мерцаетъ призрачная сцена,
Хоры слабые тѣней,
Захлеснула шелкомъ Мельпомена
Окна храмины своей.
Чернымъ таборомъ стоятъ кареты,
На дворѣ морозъ трещитъ,
Все космато: люди и предметы,
И горячій снѣгъ хруститъ.

2

Понемногу челядь разбираетъ
Шубъ медвѣжьихъ吧 вороха,
Въ суматохѣ бабочка летаетъ,
Розу кутаютъ въ мѣха.
Модной пестряди кружки и мошки,
Театральный легкій жаръ,
А на улицѣ мигаютъ плошки,
И тяжелый валитъ паръ.

3

Кучера измаялись отъ крика,
И кромѣшна ночи тьма,
Ничего, голубка Эвридика,
Что у насъ студеная зима.
Слаще пѣнья итальянской рѣчи
Для меня родной языкъ,
Ибо въ немъ таинственно лепечетъ
Чужеземныхъ арфъ родникъ.

4

Пахнетъ дымомъ бѣдная овчина,
Отъ сугроба улица черна,
Изъ блаженнаго, пѣвучаго притона
Къ намъ летитъ безсмертная весна,
Чтобы вѣчно арія звучала
„Ты вернешься на зеленые луга“ —
И живая ласточка упала
На горячіе снѣга.

1

A phantom scene barely glimmers,
The soft choruses of shades,
Melpomene [25] has lashed the windows of her room with silk.
Wagons stand in the black gypsy-camp.
The frost crackles in the courtyard.
Everything is dishevelled—people and objects,
The burning snow crunches.

2

Piece by piece, the servants take down
Piles of bearskin coats.
In the rummage of a butterfly,
A rose muffled in the fur.
Moths and money boxes of colorful linen,
A light theatrical fire.
On the street the lamps flicker,
And the heavy steam gathers.

3

The coachmen are weary from shouting,
The darkness heaves and snorts.
No matter, my dove Eurydice,
That our winter is bitter.
For me, my native tongue is sweeter
Than the music of Italian speech,
For in it, the fount of foreign harps
Will mysteriously stammer.

4

The pitiful sheepskin smells of smoke,
From a snow drift the street is black.
Out of the glorious melodic stream
Immortal Spring flies to us, so that
The aria eternally resounds:
"You will return to the green meadows,"
And the living swallow fell back
On the burning snow.

ВЕНИЦЕЙСКАЯ ЖИЗНЬ

1

Веницейской жизни мрачной и безплодной
Для меня значеніе свѣтло,
Вотъ она глядитъ съ улыбкою холодной
Въ голубое дряхлое стекло.

2

Тонкій воздухъ, кожи синія прожилки,
Бѣлый снѣгъ,. зеленая парча,.
Всѣхъ кладутъ на кипарисныя носилки,
Сонныхъ, теплыхъ вынимаютъ изъ плаща.

3

И горятъ, горятъ въ корзинахъ свѣчи,
Словно голубь залетѣлъ въ ковчегъ,
На театрѣ и на праздномъ вѣчѣ
Умираетъ человѣкъ.

4

Ибо нѣтъ спасенья отъ любви и страха,
Тяжелѣе платины Сатурново кольцо,
Чернымъ бархатомъ завѣшенная плаха
И прекрасное лицо.

5

Тяжелы твои, Венеція, уборы,
Въ кипарисныхъ рамахъ зеркала.
Воздухъ твой граненый. Въ спальнѣ таютъ горы
Голубого, дряхлаго стекла.

6

Только въ пальцахъ роза или склянка.
Адріатика зеленая, прости,
Что же ты молчишь, скажи, венеціанка?
Какъ отъ этой смерти праздничной уйти?

7

Черный Весперъ въ зеркалѣ мерцаетъ.
Все проходитъ. Истина темна.
Человѣкъ родится. Жемчугъ умираетъ.
И Сусанна старцевъ ждать должна.

1920

VENETIAN LIFE [26]

1

The meaning of somber and sterile
Venetian life is clear to me: here
She looks into a deep decrepit glass
With a cool smile.

2

Fine leather air. Blue veins.
White snow. Green brocade.
They are all placed on cypress stretchers,
Taken warm and drowsy from a cape.

3

And the candles burn, burn in baskets,
As if a pigeon had flown into the shrine.
At the theater and the solemn council,
A person is dying.

4

Because there is no salvation from love and fear:
Saturn's rings are heavier than platinum!
The chopping block is covered with black velvet,
And on it, a beautiful face.

5

Your jewels are heavy, Venezia,
In the cypress mirror frame.
Your air is faceted. In the bedroom,
The blue mountains of decrepit glass dissolve.

6

Only in her hands are the rose and the hourglass—
Green Adriatic, forgive me.
Why are you silent, Venetienne,
How can I escape this solemn death.

7

Black Hesper glimmers in the mirror.
Everything passes, the truth is vague.
A man is born, a pearl dies.
And Susannah has to wait for old men.

Мнѣ жалко, что теперь зима,
И комаровъ не слышно въ домѣ,
Но ты напомнила сама
О легкомысленной соломѣ.

Стрекозы вьются въ синевѣ,
И ласточкой кружится мода,
Корзиночка на головѣ —
Или напыщенная ода?

Совѣтовать я не берусь,
И безполезны отговорки,
Но взбитыхъ сливокъ вѣченъ вкусъ
И запахъ апельсинной корки.

Ты все толкуешь наобумъ,
Отъ этого ничуть не хуже.
Что дѣлать: самый нѣжный умъ
Весь помѣщается снаружи.

И ты пытаешься желтокъ
Взбивать разсерженною ложкой,
Онъ побѣлѣлъ, онъ изнемогъ —
И все-таки, еще немножко...

Въ тебѣ все дразнитъ, все поетъ,
Какъ итальянская рулада.
И маленькій вишневый ротъ
Сухого проситъ винограда.

Такъ не старайся быть умнѣй,
Въ тебѣ все прихоть, все минута,
Въ тѣни отъ шапочки твоей
Венеціанская баута.

Декабрь 1920

I am sorry it is winter now,
And you can't hear gnats in the house.
But you remind yourself
Of the light-headed straw.

The dragonflies hover in the blue sky,
And fashion turns around like a swallow;
A basket on the head,
Or a bombastic ode?

I won't endeavor to give advice
And useless excuses,
But the taste of whipped cream
And the smell of oranges lasts forever.

You define everything without thinking,
And by doing no worse,
The most sensitive mind
Is put wholly outside.

You attempt to beat the yolk
With an angry spoon.
It grew white, it succumbed.
And yet there's still a little more. [27]

In you everything provokes, everything sings
Like an Italian roulade,
And a small cherry mouth
Demands a dry vineyard.

Do not take such pains to be wise,
In you everything is whimsy,
And the shadow from your cap—
A Venetian *bautta*. [28]

Вотъ дароносица, какъ солнце золотое
Повисла въ воздухѣ — великолѣпный мигъ.
Здѣсь долженъ прозвучать лишь греческій языкъ:
Взять въ руки цѣлый міръ, какъ яблоко простое.

Богослуженія торжественный зенитъ,
Свѣтъ въ круглой храминѣ подъ куполомъ въ іюлѣ,
Чтобъ полной грудью мы внѣ времени вздохнули
О луговинѣ той, гдѣ время не бѣжитъ.

И Евхаристія, какъ вѣчный полдень длится —
Всѣ причащаются, играютъ и поютъ,
И на виду у всѣхъ божественный сосудъ
Неисчерпаемымъ веселіемъ струится.

The chalice was suspended in the air
Like the golden sun for a golden moment.
Here it is proper for only Greek to be heard:
To take in its hands the whole world, like a simple apple.

The triumphal zenith of the divine service,
Light in a round room under a cupola in July,
That we could sigh with a heavy chest
About that meadow beyond time, where time doesn't fly.

The Eucharist drags on like an eternal noon—
Everyone takes the Sacrament, performs, and sings,
In view of everyone the sacred vessel
Pours out with inexhaustible rejoicing.

Когда Психея-жизнь спускается къ тѣнямъ
Въ полупрозрачный лѣсъ вослѣдъ за Персефоной,
Слѣпая ласточка бросается къ ногамъ
Съ стигійской нѣжностью и вѣткою зеленой.

Навстрѣчу бѣженкѣ спѣшитъ толпа тѣней,
Товарку новую встрѣчая причитаньемъ,
И руки слабыя ломаютъ передъ ней
Съ недоумѣніемъ и робкимъ упованьемъ.

Кто держитъ зеркало, кто баночку духовъ;
Душа вѣдь женщина, ей нравятся бездѣлки,
И лѣсъ безлиственный прозрачныхъ голосовъ
Сухія шалости кропятъ, какъ дождикъ мелкій.

И въ нѣжной сутолкѣ не зная, что начать,
Душа не узнаетъ прозрачныя дубравы,
Дохнетъ на зеркало и медлитъ передать
Лепешку мѣдную съ туманной переправы.

As Psyche-Life goes down to the shades
In a translucent forest in Persephone's tracks,
A blind swallow falls at her feet
With Stygian tenderness and a green branch.

The shades flock to meet the fugitive,
Welcome their new visitor with weeping,
Wring their feeble hands before her
Bewildered and in timid hope.

One holds a mirror, another a phial of perfume—
The soul is a woman, fond of trifles
And the leafless forest is sprinkled with fine rain of
Laments, dry transparent voices.

And in the gentle confusion, not knowing where to start,
She does not recognize the spectral wood,
And breathes on the mirror, holds the
Copper coin for the misty crossing.

Возьми на радость изъ моихъ ладоней
Немного солнца и немного меда,
Какъ намъ велѣли пчелы Персефоны.

Не отвязать неприкрѣпленной лодки,
Не услыхать въ мѣха обутой тѣни,
Не превозмочь въ дремучей жизни страха.

Намъ остаются только поцѣлуи,
Мохнатые, какъ маленькія пчелы,
Что умираютъ, вылетѣвъ изъ улья.

Они шуршатъ въ прозрачныхъ дебряхъ ночи,
Ихъ родина дремучій лѣсъ Тайгета,
Ихъ пища — время, медуница, мята.

Возьми жъ на радость дикій мой подарокъ —
Невзрачное сухое ожерелье
Изъ мертвыхъ пчелъ, медъ превратившихъ въ солнце.

Just for joy, take from my palms
A little sun, a little honey,
As Persephone's bees have commanded.

An unfastened boat cannot be untied.
A spirit in shoes walking through furs cannot be heard.
In the thick forest of life fear cannot be overcome.

Only kisses are left for us.
Furry, like small bees
That die when they leave the hive.

They buzz in transparent thickets of night,
Their habitat is the dense Taiga woods;
Their food—time, honeysuckle, mint.

So take for joy my passionate gift,
A dry, unsightly necklace
Of dead bees, who changed honey into sun.

СУМЕРКИ СВОБОДЫ.

1

Прославимъ, братья, сумерки свободы,
Великій сумеречный годъ.
Въ кипящія ночныя воды
Опущенъ грузный лѣсъ тенетъ.
Восходишь ты въ глухіе годы,
О, солнце, судія-народъ.

2

Прославимъ роковое бремя,
Которое въ слезахъ народный вождь беретъ.
Прославимъ власти сумрачное бремя,
Ея невыносимый гнетъ.
Въ комъ сердце есть, тотъ долженъ слышать, время,
Какъ твой корабль ко дну идетъ.

3

Мы въ легіоны боевые
Связали ласточекъ, и вотъ
Не видно солнца, вся стихія
Щебечетъ, движется, живетъ,
Сквозь сѣти сумерки густыя
Не видно солнца, и земля плыветъ.

4

Ну, что жъ, попробуемъ: огромный, неуклюжій,
Скрипучій поворотъ руля.
Земля плыветъ.   Мужайтесь, мужи,
Какъ плугомъ, океанъ дѣля,
Мы будемъ помнить и въ летейской стужѣ,
Что десяти небесъ намъ стоила земля.

THE TWILIGHT OF FREEDOM

1

Let us glorify, brothers, the twilight of freedom—
The great setting year.
A weighty forest of nets is lowered
Into the bubbling waters of night.
You are rising into barren years,
O sun, judge, people.

2

Let us glorify the burden of fate,
Which in time of tears takes the nation's helm.
Let us glorify the dark burden of power,
Its unbearable oppression.
Whoever has the heart should learn, time,
How your ship is sinking.

3

We tied the swallows into battle legions
And so, the sun's obscured; the whole element
Warbles, whirls, lives;
Through the nets—a dense twilight—
The sun's obscured, and the land sets sail.

4

But still, let us try: an enormous, awkward,
Screeching turn of the wheel.
The land is sailing. Take courage, men!
Dividing the water, like a plow,
We will recall even in Lethe's frost,
That our land was worth ten heavens.

1

На страшной высотѣ блуждающій огонь,
Но развѣ такъ звѣзда мерцаетъ?
Прозрачная звѣзда, блуждающій огонь,
Твой братъ, Петрополь, умираетъ.

2

На страшной высотѣ земные сны горятъ,
Зеленая звѣзда летаетъ.
О, если ты звѣзда,—воды и неба братъ,
Твой братъ, Петрополь, умираетъ.

3

Чудовищный корабль на страшной высотѣ
Несется, крылья расправляетъ.
Зеленая звѣзда, въ прекрасной нищетѣ
Твой братъ, Петрополь, умираетъ.

4

Прозрачная весна надъ черною Невой
Сломалась. Воскъ безсмертья таетъ.
О, если ты звѣзда—Петрополь, городъ твой,
Твой братъ, Петрополь, умираетъ.

1

At a dreadful height, a wandering fire—
But does a star really flicker like that?
Transparent star, wandering fire,
Your brother, Petropolis, is dying.

2

At a dreadful height, earthly dreams are burning,
A green star is twinkling.
O if you, star, are the brother of water and sky,
Your brother, Petropolis, is dying.

3

A monstrous ship flies at a dreadful height,
Spreading its wings—
Green star, in beautiful poverty
Your brother, Petropolis, is dying.

4

Above the black Neva, transparent Spring
Is smashed, the wax of immortality is melting.
O if you, star, are Petropolis, your city,
your brother, Petropolis, is dying.

ЛАСТОЧКА.

1

Я слово позабылъ, что я хотѣлъ сказать:
Слѣпая ласточка въ чертогъ тѣней вернется
На крыльяхъ срѣзанныхъ съ прозрачными играть.
Въ безпамятствѣ ночная пѣснь поется.

2

Не слышно птицъ. Безсмертникъ не цвѣтетъ,
Прозрачны гривы табуна ночного,
Въ сухой рѣкѣ пустой челнокъ плыветъ,
Среди кузнечиковъ безпамятствуетъ слово.

3

И медленно растетъ какъ бы шатеръ иль храмъ,
То вдругъ прикинется безумной Антигоной,
То мертвой ласточкой бросается къ ногамъ
Съ стигійской нѣжностью и вѣткою зеленой.

4

О, если бы вернуть и зрячихъ пальцевъ стыдъ,
И выпуклую радость узнаванья,
Я такъ боюсь рыданья Аонидъ,
Тумана, звона и зіянья.

5

А смертнымъ власть дана любить и узнавать,
Для нихъ и звукъ въ персты прольется,
Но я забылъ, что я хочу сказать,
И мысль безплотная въ чертогъ тѣней вернется.

6

Все не о томъ прозрачная твердитъ,
Все ласточка, подружка, Антигона, . . .
А на губахъ, какъ черный ледъ, горитъ
Стигійскаго воспоминанье звона.

1920

SWALLOW

1

I have forgotten the word that I wanted to say.
On clipped wings the blind swallow will return
To the hall of shadows, to play with the shades.
A night song is sung in forgetfulness.

2

The bird cannot be heard. The immortelle does not bloom.
A herd of night mares with transparent manes.
An empty canoe glides on a waterless river.
Among the grasshoppers the word becomes forgotten.

3

And it grows slowly, like a temple or tent,
And suddenly, like crazed Antigone, falls on its side,
Lands at the feet, like a dead swallow,
With Stygian tenderness and a green branch.

4

O, if I could give back the disgrace of
Fingers that see and the clear joy of recognition.
I am so afraid of the Aonides' [29] weeping,
Of mist, ringing, the abyss.

5

Yet the power to love and perceive is given to mortals,
For them even the sound spreads to their fingers,
But I forgot what I want to say,
The intangible thought returns to the hall of shadows.

6

The transparency always repeats the word,
Always: swallow, friend, Antigone...
But on the lips, like black ice, burns
The remembrance of a Stygian sound.

За то, что я руки твои не сумѣлъ удержать,
За то, что я предалъ соленыя нѣжныя губы,
Я долженъ разсвѣта въ дремучемъ акрополѣ ждать.
Какъ я ненавижу плакучіе древніе срубы.

Ахейскіе мужи во тьмѣ снаряжаютъ коня,
Зубчатыми пилами въ стѣны вгрызаются крѣпко,
Никакъ не уляжется крови сухая возня,
И нѣтъ для тебя ни названія, ни звука, ни слѣпка.

Какъ могъ я подумать, что ты возвратишься, какъ
                                смѣлъ!
Зачѣмъ преждевременно я отъ тебя оторвался!
Еще не разсѣялся мракъ, и пѣтухъ не пропѣлъ,
Еще въ древесину горячій топоръ не врѣзался.

Прозрачной слезой на стѣнахъ проступила смола,
И чувствуетъ городъ свои деревянныя ребра,
Но хлынула къ лѣстницамъ кровь и на приступъ
                                пошла,
И трижды приснился мужамъ соблазнительный
                                образъ.

Гдѣ милая Троя, гдѣ царскій, гдѣ дѣвичій домъ?
Онъ будетъ разрушенъ, высокій Пріамовъ сково-
                                рѣшникъ.
И падаютъ стрѣлы сухимъ деревяннымъ дождемъ,
И стрѣлы другія растутъ на землѣ, какъ орѣшникъ.

Послѣдней звѣзды безболѣзненно гаснетъ уколъ,
И сѣрою ласточкой утро въ окно постучится,
И медленный день, какъ въ соломѣ проснувшійся
                                волъ
На стогнахъ шершавыхъ отъ долгаго сна шевелится.

Декабрь 1920

If I am to know how to restrain your hands,
If I am to relinquish the tender, salty lips,
I must wait for daybreak in the dense acropolis.
How I hate those ancient weeping willows.

Achaian men equip their steeds in darkness.
With jagged saws they rip firmly into the walls.
The dry noise of blood does not subside at all,
And for you there is no sound, no name, no mold.

How daring it was to think you would return!
For what were we separated so prematurely!
The gloom has still not dispersed,
The cock has not finished his song,
The glowing axe has still not entered the wood.

The resin came forth on the walls like a transparent tear,
And the city feels its wooden ribs,
But the blood rushed out to the stairs, went on the attack,
And thrice the men dreamed of the tempting figure.

Where is pleasant Troy, where is the king's, the maiden's home?
Priam's great starling coop will be destroyed,
And the arrows will fall as a dry forest rain,
And more will spring up like a hazel grove.

The last star's sting will be extinguished painlessly,
And morning will knock on the window like a grey swallow,
Slow day will begin to stir, like an ox in the haystack
Just awakened from a long dream.

Исакій подъ фатой молочной бѣлизны
Стоитъ сѣдою голубятней,
И посохъ бередитъ сѣдыя тишины
И чинъ воздушный сердцу внятный.

Столѣтнихъ панихидъ блуждающій призрáкъ,
Широкій выносъ плащаницы,
И въ ветхомъ неводѣ генисаретскій мракъ
Великопостныя седмицы.

Ветхозавѣтный дымъ на теплыхъ алтаряхъ
И іерея возгласъ сирый,
Смиренникъ царственный: снѣгъ чистый на плечахъ
И одичалыя порфиры.

Соборы вѣчные Софіи и Петра,
Амбары воздуха и свѣта,
Зернохранилища вселенскаго добра,
И риги новаго завѣта.

Не къ вамъ влечется духъ въ годины тяжкихъ бѣдъ,
Сюда влачится по ступенямъ
Широкопасмурнымъ несчастья волчій слѣдъ,
Ему вовѣки не измѣнимъ.

Зане свободенъ рабъ, преодолѣвшій страхъ,
И сохранилось свыше мѣры
Въ прохладныхъ житницахъ, въ глубокихъ закромахъ
Зерно глубокой, полной вѣры.

1921.

Beneath a veil of milky white
Stands Isaac's [30] like a hoary dovecote,
The crozier irritates the grey silences,
The heart understands the airy rite.

The wandering spectre of the centennial requiem,
The grand bearing of the shroud
And in a worn-out seine, the Gennesarian [31] gloom
Of the Lenten Week.

The Old Testament smoke on warm altars,
And the final, orphaned cry [32] of the priest,
A regal, humble man: clean snow on his shoulders,
And the savage purple mantles.

The eternal cathedrals of Sofia and Peter,
Storehouses of air and light, the possessions
Of the ecumenical granary
And the barn of the New Testament.

The spirit is not drawn to you in sorely troubled times,
Here drags the wolf's track of unhappiness
Along the cloudy steps;
We will never change it:

For the slave is free, fear is overcome,
And preserved beyond measure
In the cool granaries, in deep combines,
Is the kernel of deep, full faith.

NOTES TO THE POEMS

1. The scene here is most likely taken from Racine's Phedre, (*'Que ces vains ornements, que ces voiles me pèsent.'*) and not directly from Euripides' *Hippolytus*. See *Phedre*, Sc. III.

2. *Uglich:* on the import of Uglich, see Clarence Brown's *Mandelstam:* 'Uglich' is as familiar a name, and almost as fraught with his meaning, as 'Runnymede,' say, or the 'Alamo,' (p. 222).

3. An allusion to the Time of Troubles (1598-1613) in Russia, from the rule of Boris Godunov to that of Mikhail Fyodorovich Romanov. Basically, this poem concerns Theodore's half-brother, Dmitri Tsarevich, who in 1591 was found in the courtyard of his estate in Uglich, a small town outside of Moscow, with throat mysteriously slashed, thus paving the way for a dynastic crisis.

4. *three meetings:* the Metropolitan of Moscow was consecrated as the Third Rome in 1589, under Theodore I. It is conjectured that the reason for this was that "those who formulated [the doctine] believed the end of the world was approaching and the Last Judgment. They were merely trying to keep Orthodox Christianity alive as a last refuge to the end." (G. Vernadsky, *A History of Russia*)

5. *bound hands:* it is believed that Dmitri was an epileptic

6. *Solominka:* Princess Salomeia Nikolaevna Andronikova, or, as she was better known in Western Europe, Lou-Andreas Salome.

7. *Salamis:* Ajax accompanied the Greeks with twelve Salaminian ships to the Trojan War.

8. *medusa:* here, since it is not capitalized, can mean either a generalized Medusa, snakes and all, or a sea-nettle or type of jellyfish.

9. *Taurides:* a mountain range in Turkey near the Black Sea. See also the poem beginning "The thick golden stream of honey..." (p.35)

10. *"Baiu, baiushki, baiu...":* the beginning of a well-known Russian lullaby.

11. *Quadrigae:* L., 'four-horsed chariots.'

12. *What?/Was?* (Russ. *Shto?/Vo?:*): in the Struve & Filippov edition, these lines begin "Shto?"/"Tso" which are different pronunciations of the word for 'what' in Russian and Polish (or Ukrainian), respectively. "Vo," on the other hand, might also be a cyrillicization of German "Wo," 'where.' [In any case, Mandelstam is suggesting a difference in dialect or language between two speakers.]

¹³ wax: a Slavic method of divination was the spilling of molten wax or lead into cold water. Its final, cooled-off shape would then be interpreted.

¹⁴ Pierius: a mountain in NE Greece, said to be the first place known where the muses were worshipped.

¹⁵ little song: "In the Blacksmith's Shop"

¹⁶ Epirus: a region in western Greece.

¹⁷ In the Struve edition of Mandelstam's works these stanzas are included as the concluding lines (25-40) of the poem printed below:

[111]
Theodosia *

Surrounded by high hills, you
Run down from the mountain with a herd of sheep,
And you sparkle in the dry, clear air
Like rosy, white stones.
The pirate *feluccas* flounder, the poppies
Of Turkish flags seem to burn in the port,
And the reeds of masts, the elastic crystal of the wave,
And skiff-hammocks hanging on the ropes.

And in all ways, from morning till night
and cried over by everyone, "Yablochko" is sung.
The wind carries away the golden seed—
It was lost, never to return.
But in the alleys, just become dark,
the incapable musicians, huddled in twos and threes,
Begin to sing their improbable variations.

O figures of hook-nosed travellers,
This joyous Mediterranean menagery!
The Turks in their towels wander about
Like chickens at a little inn.
They transport dogs in prison-like wagons,
The dry dust on the streets flies up,
And indifferent among the bazaar fury
Is a monumental cook from a battle ship.

* A resort in the Crimea, where Mandelstam lived in 1919.

¹⁸ world: the Russian word for 'world' is the same as the word for peace: mir.

¹⁹ Assumption, Archangel, Resurrection: cathedrals in Moscow.

²⁰ Kypris: Aphrodite (of Cyprus, one of the chief seats of worship of that goddess).

²¹ Sazandar: a musician; a member of the National Ensembles of Azerbaijan, Armenia, Georgia, Iran.

²² *Kura*: a river in the Caucasus mountains.

²³ *Dukhan*: a Caucasian inn. A *dukhanshchik* is apparently a waiter at one of the inns.

²⁴ In the Struve edition this stanza is included as the concluding lines of the poem:

> A man grows old.
> But a lamb, young,
> And under the narrow moon,
> With the vapor of rose wine,
> Flies a shashlik thought.

²⁵ *Melpomene*: the Muse of Tragedy.

²⁶ This poem most likely refers to one of the many paintings of Susannah in the Bath or with the elders done by Renaissance artists. The story itself is in the Old Testament Apocrypha.

²⁷ In the Struve edition the following lines are included as the sixth stanza of the poem:

> Justice, it's not your fault, really,
> So why the appraisals and reverses?
> You are so purposely created
> For comical mutual quarrel.

²⁸ *bautta*: It., 'a black cape with a hood or mask; a cowl.'

²⁹ *Aonides*: the Muses, so-called because Mt. Helicon and the fountain of Aganippe were in Aonia.

³⁰ *St. Isaac*: a cathedral in St. Petersburg (Leningrad).

³¹ *Gennesarian*: Gennesar, or Gennesaret, is a biblical town or region N.W. of the Sea of Galilee. It is mentioned in I Maccabees, as well as Luke 5:1, Matthew 14:34, and Mark 6:53. The New Testament reference follows Jesus' walking on water. Perhaps the gloom Mandelstam is describing derives from the following scene: "...they came into the land of Gennesaret. And when the men of that place had knowledge of him, they sent out into all that country round about, and brought unto him all that were diseased; And ran through that whole region round about, and began to carry about in beds those that were sick..."

³² *cry* (Russian, *'vozglas'*): no English word can translate this word accurately; it means, roughly, "the final notes of a prayer which are sung or chanted in a loud voice." An alternate translation of this line might be: 'And the orphaned final notes of the priest."

TRANSLATOR'S NOTE

I am glad that these translations are at last illuminated by the intense rays of Mandelstam's exquisite originals. Glad, of course, that in facing their source, they may bask, may even be elucidated as *English* poems. I am apprehensive too, for now they may be examined under sufficient light to detect the flaws that distinguish them as imitations.

Mandelstam is worth the risk. His place in Russian literature (different, to be sure, from his place in Soviet literature) demands at the very least that complete translations of his primary published texts be made available in English.

This volume provides a *complete*, bilingual edition of a collection of poems as they were published during the poet's own lifetime. As one of Osip Mandelstam's translators, and by implication, devotees, it strikes me as almost incomprehensible that Mandelstam's public fate has been such that the unavailability of a major work, *Tristia*, can have continued for so long.

Imagine, if you can, that a bilingual edition of Rilke's *Sonnets to Orpheus* had not appeared until some fifty years after the poet's death! And yet, Mandelstam is no more difficult to appreciate than Rilke, whose major books have enjoyed—or suffered, in some cases—continual retranslation, often published facing the original texts, over the years of his renown. And it would not be particularly controversial to suggest that Mandelstam's contribution to Russian literature is as great as Rilke's to German, even European, poetry.

The problem, as I have rather unscientifically discerned it over the years [many of the translations presented here were first drafted in 1971], seems to orginate from two rather hard-to-shake general notions concerning Mandelstam and his poetry: first, his books are impossible to get; second, his poetry is too difficult to understand.

Unfortunately, both of these disserving notions are rooted in some truth. The history of the publication of Mandelstam's work from its very beginnings is somewhat confused. Mandelstam's earliest and chief advocate in English, Clarence Brown, describes the situation thus:

> Mandelstam published two books of poetry, or two and a half, or three, depending upon how you wish to regard a special section of poems that appeared in the collection of 1928. The first was *Kamen'* (Stone), the second *Tristia*. And when these appeared under their original titles within the collection *Stikhotvoreniia* (Poems) of 1928, Mandelstam printed twenty poems under the rubric '1921-1925.'

> These books appeared in various editions, under various
> names, and—what is somewhat more surprising and
> confusing—with a varied composition of poems. [*Man-
> delstam*, p. 159]

For readers in the West, the problem in one sense was alleviated by the publication of the three volumes of Collected Works completed in 1971 by editors Gleb Struve and Boris Filippov. In fact, when I and many others first got our hands on Mandelstam, the Struve and Filippov version was almost canonical, because it was next to impossible to obtain a copy of the orginal edition.

At the same time, more confusion was added because the poems that comprised the Struve/Filippov *Tristia* did not correspond to the set in the original *Tristia*, published in Berlin in 1922. The first edition was actually arranged and entitled by the poet/publisher Mikhail Kuzmin, and Osip Mandelstam himself was not entirely satisfied with the final selection.

From an historical point of view, the first edition of Man-delstam's "second book" (which, by the way, *Tristia* was named in the subsequent, 1923 edition) is the best we have. It is the text chosen by the late Carl Proffer for the Ardis Press facsimile edition (now out-of-print), and it is the text supplied for this bilingual edition. The slight inconvenience of the typographic differences, which can easily be overcome, may be compensated for by the authenticity of the text.

A confusing publication history, however, while providing grist for some future editor's mill, is not the only force at work in keep-ing alive the sense that Mandelstam is unavailable. Much has been written about the politics and biographical issues behind this sad state of affairs. For my part I wish simply to narrate three somewhat telling personal experiences for the light they may shed on the problem.

The first took place some time ago, the mid-Seventies, to the best of my recollection, in the Four Continents bookstore (now Victor Kamkin) in New York. This particular bookstore had a reasonably good selection of Soviet published editions of literature, science, technology, art, criticism, what have you, and it was clearly supplied directly by the Soviets. After browsing naively quite some time in the literature and poetry shelves, I approached the snide and supercilious, Nabokovian bookseller, and in my best student Russian, asked where I might find works by Mandelstam. Not deigning to respond to me in Russian, he said, after a haughty silence, "You might look over there, but we don't have much in our Jewish section."

Some years later—1982, to be exact—in Moscow—I noticed that an Intourist interpreter was reading the Russian poet Aleksandr Blok on the bus. A brief conversation with her about modern Russian poetry led me to mention that I had translated Mandelstam. A strange, anxious look came over her face, and she said, "Oh, but he's so *difficult*" as if she were impressed that a foreigner had tackled him. "Oh," I said, "you have read him?" "No," she replied.

And now, thirty years after the first collection of Mandelstam in Russian was made available in the West by Struve and Filippov, the following: a proposal for research at Moscow State University is kicked back at me not because of the unsuitability of the topic, but rather because my *anketa*—a sort of proposal-cum-vita—includes the fact that I have translated Mandelstam. I am called by MSU administrators a "provocateur."

Politico-historical "accidents" have somehow conspired to prevent the sort of free circulation of source texts that one generally expects so long after the death of a major literary figure. Despite Mandelstam's reputation for abstruseness, it would still be a mistake for anyone in the West to assume that the work is in any sense "impenetrable." On the contrary: as the most important representative of a poetic movement called Acmeism, which demanded above all else clarity (as against the vague mysticism of the Russian Symbolists), Mandelstam at his best is precise, clear, totally present within the poem.

At the same time, he does not condescend; he does not popularize or simplify grand poetic themes. He found such practice abhorrent:

> The whole tragedy arises when, instead of the real past with
> its deep roots, we get "yesterday"...easily understood poetry,
> a cosy little corner. ["An Acmeist Manifesto"]

By focusing upon the solidity inherent in the language itself, he is able to contain the metaphysical within beautiful, religious spaces. And his obvious affection for things and words Russian; for classical, Hellenic themes; for church architecture—these and other attentions naturally enough inform his writing to the extent that one must try to be aware of at least the explicit references and allusions in order to apprehend the poem most fully.

For their part, my own annotations serve as a sort of minimum of "background information" for the reader totally unacquainted with Mandelstam and his culture. The reader wishing to examine Mandelstam more thoroughly would do well to take up quickly both Clarence Brown's *Mandelstam* and the memoirs of the poet's wife Nadezhda Mandelstam, entitled *Hope Against Hope*.

It is my sincere desire that the publication of this edition will contribute to the continuing effort to establish for this great modern Russian poet a reputation founded upon thorough familiarity with the work itself, rather than upon hearsay and criticism. As this reputation grows, perhaps, as occurred just recently with Nabokov, the literary legislators in Mandelstam's own homeland (and let us not forget that *Tristia* was the title of Ovid's memoirs from exile) may soon have to overcome their embarrassment, and admit, by publishing his works, that it is useless to deny that great literature is what it is.

SELECTED BIBLIOGRAPHY

In Russian:

Sobranie sochinenii (Collected Works), 3 vols. Edited by Gleb Struve and Boris Filippov. New York: Inter-Language Literary Associates, 1964-1971.

Kamen' (Stone). St. Petersburg: Akme, 1913. Facsimile edition, Ann Arbor, Michigan: Ardis Publishers, 1971.

Tristia. Petersburg-Berlin, 1922. Facsimile edition, Ann Arbor, Michigan: Ardis Publishers, 1972.

Stikhotvoreniia (Poems). Edited by A. L. Dymshitz and N. I. Khardzhiev. Leningrad: Sovetskii Pisatel', 1974.

In English:

Osip Mandelstam's Stone. Translated and Introduced by Robert Tracy. Princeton, New Jersey: Princeton University Press, 1981.

The Prose of Osip Mandelstam. Translated, with a critical essay, by Clarence Brown. Princeton, New Jersey: Princeton University Press, 1967.

Selected Poems. A bilingual edition, translated by David McDuff. New York: Farrar, Strauss, & Giroux, 1975.

Tristia. Translated by Bruce McClelland. In: *The Silver Age of Russian Culture.* Edited by Carl Proffer. Ann Arbor, Michigan: Ardis Publishers, 1975.

Biography:

Brown, Clarence, *Mandelstam.* Cambridge: Cambridge Univ. Press, 1973.

Mandelstam, Nadezhda Yakovlevna. *Hope Against Hope: A Memoir.* New York: Atheneum, 1970.

INDEX TO FIRST LINES AND TITLES